WRITE
From the Start

WRITE
From the Start

A guide for teachers to teach writing
and for struggling students to learn how to write.

Lakesha Parson, Ed. S.

outskirtspress
DENVER, COLORADO

Write From the Start
A Guide for Teachers to Teach Writing and for Struggling Students to Learn How to Write

Outskirts Press, Inc.
http://www.outskirtspress.com

ISBN: 978-1-4327-8241-2

Outskirts Press and the "OP" logo are trademarks belonging to Outskirts Press, Inc.

PRINTED IN THE UNITED STATES OF AMERICA

Introduction

How often have teachers gotten students in the upper grades and they didn't have early writing skills? How many times have teachers not known where to start to teach a student to write from where they are? As educators, we only teach students the 5-step writing process instead of teaching them "how" to write. It's important that children learn early that stories have a beginning, middle, and ending. Young children should know they are writing even when they are scribbling. In this book students and teachers will have a tool that lays a foundation for writing and guides them to building on that foundation.

Dedication

For my son, my motivation and inspiration. I am proud I was chosen to be your mother. Words can't express the love I have for you.

For my colleagues who struggle with teaching children "how" to write, you no longer have to "create" your own writing textbook. Take care of yourselves and nourish your teaching abilities!

Table of Contents

Why is Writing Important?

Practical- Most of us create lists, jot down reminders, write notes, diary entries, send text messages, & instructions at least occasionally.

Job Related- Professional and white collar workers write frequently—preparing memos, letters, proposals, sales reports, research reports, and articles. Most workers do "some" writing on the job. Even before you get a job, you write to fill out the application and to prepare a resume.

- Teachers complete lesson plans & notes to parents
- Physicians, doctors, nurses, & pharmacists write prescriptions
- Attorneys write briefings
- Rappers write raps
- Singers and song writers write songs
- Authors write books
- Poets write poetry
- Writers write articles, songs, raps, & all sorts of other things

Stimulating- Writing helps to provoke thoughts and to organize them logically and concisely.

Social- Most of us write thank-you notes and letters to friends at least every now and then.

Therapeutic- It can be helpful to express feelings in writing that cannot be expressed so easily by speaking.

Things a parent can do at home to create a supportive environment that encourages writing

- Talk with your child about places you visit, work you do, books you read, or television programs you watch together.

- Praise your child's efforts at writing. Be primarily interested in content. Emphasize your child's successes. For every error your child makes, there are a dozen things done well. Try not to focus only on errors of spelling, punctuation, and other mechanical parts of writing.

- Provide a suitable place for your child to write—a flat surface, good light, a comfortable chair.

- Encourage your child to write and create things for fun. Some things they can write and create are travel brochures, menus, letters, poems, plays, telephone messages, or notes to family members.

- Give gifts associated with writing: pens, pencils, notepads or paper, stationery, a dictionary or thesaurus, erasers-even stamps.

Tips for Parents to Encourage Student Writing

- Coach- Don't write for your child. Question, listen, and talk about writing together. Students should do their own drafting, revising, and editing with you assisting and coaching.

- Listen attentively as your child reads their writing to you.

- Encourage the youngest writers to "read" their writing aloud whether it is scribbles, drawings, or strings of letters. Talk about the story.

- Go places and see things with your child. Then talk about what has been seen, heard, smelled, tasted, and touched. The basis of good writing is good talk. Younger children especially grow into stronger control of language when adults, especially parents, share experiences and rich talk about those experiences.

- Let your child SEE you write.

- Share your own writing and ask for their feedback.

- Share letters from friends and relatives.

What a kindergarten student should know and be able to do

- Scribbles and draws a picture to express a message.

- The sentence they write should be about the picture.

- Your student should be able to read what he or she has written even if it is only scribbles.

- Uses inventive spelling by using one or more consonants (initial/final sounds)

A kindergartner's sentence: Th dg ws bkg owtsd.

Actual Sentence: The dog was barking outside.

What a first grader should know and be able to do

- Begin to develop topics

- Writes multiple sentences about the same topic

- Uses complete thoughts

- Create stories with a beginning and an end

- Uses upper and lower case letters correctly

- Use periods, question marks, and exclamation marks

- Should be able to write at least 3 sentences

First graders can write about a particular person or object. They should be able to tell what the object has, feels, and can do.

A first grader's object: Doll

A first grader can tell what the doll has, how it looks, and what it can do.

The verbs can connect the object or person; has, looks, and can.

Doll has hair.
Doll looks pretty.
Doll can sing.

The teacher can model to the students that doll can be replaced with the pronoun she or her. The teacher will guide the student in telling more about what the doll has, how she looks, and what she can do by adding the word *and*.

Doll has clothes and hair.
She looks pretty and skinny.
Doll can sing and talk.

Use the graphic organizer shown to brainstorm

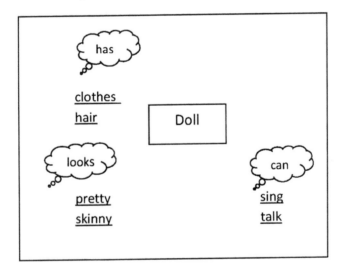

What a second grader should know and be able to do

- Writes so that the topic is clear

- Writes in a focused and logical sequence including a beginning, middle, and end

- Uses upper and lower cases correctly

- Uses ending marks and capitalization correctly

- Writes for a variety of purposes

Prompt: Write about the best birthday you ever had.

Brainstorm: Think about the best birthday you ever had. Think about where it was, who came to the party, or what you did.

Use the graphic organizers shown to brainstorm

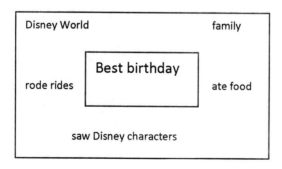

Plan: Now plan your writing.

Students should:

Tell when they went to Disney World i.e., last summer, last year, June 1, three years ago

Tell which family members went i.e., mom, dad, sister, brother

Tell which ride was ridden i.e., roller coaster, bumper cars, water slide

Tell what food was eaten i.e. corn dog, nachos, funnel cake

Tell which Disney character was seen i.e. Mickey Mouse, Donald Duck, Winnie the Pooh

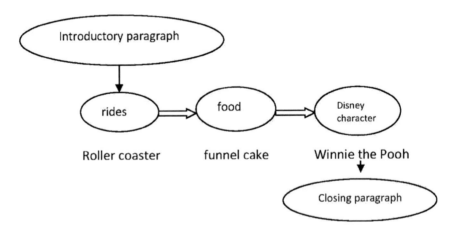

What a third grader should know and be able to do

- Writes so that the topic is clear and well developed

- Writes in a focused and logical sequence including a beginning, middle, and end

- Uses upper and lower cases correctly and can self edit

- Uses prewriting strategies like graphic organizers

- Uses details and descriptive words in writing

- Writes for a variety of purposes

What a fourth grader should know and be able to do

- Writes so that the topic is clear and well developed with a clear and well developed beginning, middle, and ending

- Uses varied language and sentence patterns effectively

- Uses prewriting strategies such as graphic organizers

- Revises and edits to improve content, punctuation, spelling, and capitalization

- Uses a variety of purposes for writing

- Uses sequence phrases to show concepts of time and order

- Uses paragraphs to organize information

- Begins the story with something interesting that will get the reader "hooked"

- Begin and end with a question, extraordinary fact, dialogue, or suspense

What a fifth grader should know and be able to do

- Writes a topic that is fully elaborated with rich details

- Has a beginning that grasps the reader's attention

- Errors don't interfere with meaning of content

- Uses prewriting strategies such as graphic organizers

- Revises and edits for content and conventions (spelling, punctuation, and capitalization)

- Uses a variety of purposes for writing

- Uses sequence/transitional phrases to show concepts of time and order

- Uses paragraphs to organize information

- Begins the story with something interesting that will "hook" the reader

- Begin and end with a question, extraordinary fact, dialogue, or suspense

What a good essay should include

A good narrative should:

1. Have five to six paragraphs

2. Stick to the topic

3. Use vivid verbs and descriptive words

4. Uses figurative language

5. Use correct punctuation, spelling, and grammar (**content weighs more than conventions**)

6. Uses transitional phrases that show smooth transitions from one topic to the next

The following is a five paragraph essay format to follow.

First paragraph- an introduction that includes a hook, tells **who** the story is about, **what** the character does or or will do, **when** the story takes place, **where** the story takes place, and **why** did it happen. The three main events (details) can also be stated here.

Second paragraph- a transitional phrase, the first main event (detail) of the story using 1-2 sentences, one sentence including dialogue, & one sentence using figurative language

Third paragraph- a transitional phrase, the second main event (detail) of the story using 1-2 sentences, one sentence including dialogue, & one sentence using figurative language

Fourth paragraph- a transitional phrase, the third main event (detail) of the story using 1-2 sentences, one sentence including dialogue, & one sentence using figurative language

Fifth paragraph- a closing statement (conclusion) that closes the story with a bang, tells the reader how the writer feels about the story, what the character(s) learned from their experience, asks a question, or what they may hope or wish for in the future. This paragraph can also restate the three main events.

To develop each detail/main event in a paragraph there are five essential questions to use as a guide to develop a writer's thought. Use vivid verbs and descriptive words throughout each paragraph.

1. What are you doing?

2. What were the people around you doing?

3. What were you thinking?

4. How did you and the people around you feel?

5. Can you describe the scene and what you saw?

What a Good Writer Should Never Do

Don't end a story with, "The End"

Don't end a story with, "This is the end of my story."

Don't end a story with, "I went home."

Don't end a story with, "I went to sleep."

Don't end a story with, "I went to bed."

Don't begin a story with Once upon a time....use a "hook" to grab the reader's attention!

The phrases in quotations above are things that are expected of a writer. Most students end with those common types of endings and begin with that type of beginning. A student's writing should stand out from the rest. End a story with a bang! Writers use various techniques to show how the character or characters have grown or changed in some way as a result of his or her experiences. The following are seven ways you can end a story.

End with *advice* to the reader.
Example: Never give up on your dreams!

End with a *memory*.
Example: I'll never forget the time I met Michael Jordan.

End with a *decision*.
Example: From that day on, Jaxson and I decided never to go camping alone.

End with *dialogue*.
Example: Kayla announced, "Well, I'll never do that again!"

End with a *feeling*.
Example: I could still feel my legs trembling from the thought of Prenston and Sidnie getting me caught.

End with a *question*.
Who would have guessed that Bailey and Madison was the same person?

End with a *hope* or *wish*.
I hope the next time we decide to go to Wonderland that Phillip, Kaylee, and Jaxson won't eat anything before we get on any rides.

How to "Hook" the reader from the start

What is a hook? A hook is a sentence in the first paragraph. It is usually in the first or second sentence and it draws the reader in and makes them want to continue to read the story. It should be lively and interesting. The following are four different ways to begin your story and examples for each.

Begin with an *extraordinary fact*.
Example: There are more than one million different kinds of insects!

*Be sure not to confuse a **"fact"** with an **"extraordinary fact"**. A fact and an extraordinary fact both are something that is true and can be proven. The difference is an extraordinary fact is something that is so extraordinary, that a lot of people don't already know about it. A fact is something everybody most likely knows i.e., Students go to school to learn. Everybody knows that and there is nothing extraordinary about that fact.*

Begin with *dialogue*.
Example: "We finally made it!" shouted Arthur.

Begin with *suspense*.
Example: As we walked into the creepy, vacant house we suddenly heard a strange sound that startled us.

Begin with a *question*.
How in the world did Kirsten end up on top of the hood of my car?

Sometimes a writer describes the scene to set up the story . After you have decided on what type of hook you will write, the sentences immediately following should include five additional important components; who, did what, when, where, & why. Your hook and the five components make up your introductory statement or introduction. Again the introduction is the first paragraph and it sets the stage for the story. Let's see an introductory statement below that uses suspense as the hook!

Introduction/introductory statement

It was a dark and stormy night when we quickly dashed into the nearest house we spotted. As we strolled into the creepy, vacant house we suddenly heard a strange sound that startled us. It all started last summer when my family and I were traveling to Los Angeles, California for vacation and all of a sudden ran out of gas in the middle of nowhere! Let me tell you all about.

Hook: It was a dark and stormy night when we quickly dashed into the nearest house we spotted. As we strolled into the creepy, vacant house we suddenly heard a strange sound that startled us. **Who:** My family and I; **Did what:** ran out of gas while traveling; **When:** last summer; **Where:** Los Angeles, California; **Why:** for vacation

More Catchy  Hooks

I could not believe my eyes!

I never expected...

Believe it or not the best adventure of my life started when...

The weirdest thing happened...

I've never seen anything like it.

Never in a million years...

Oh no!

Why did this have to happen to me?

Was it something I ate? Was it something I drank? Was it a wish upon a star?

You won't believe what happened to me!

I must be seeing things!

Other ways to write a catchy hook

Use a simile: My knees felt like water as we staggered in front of the class to perform our play.

Interjections: Yikes! WOW! YIPPPEEE! HOORAY!

Sound words: Poof! My dog vanished in thin air.

Set the scene: The warmth of her hand made me feel cozy, as the dripping sweat on my hands was cooled by the gentle wind from the cool breeze.

Definition: An eclipse is an obscuring of the light from one celestial body by another. It was a rare but beautiful occasion and I was lucky enough to be one of the thousands of people to see it! To be in one of the few places in the world to see such a sight was an amazing feeling and unbelievable!

Transitions

Good writers use transitions to show they are moving from one thought or event to the next. Students in primary grades use very basic transition or sequence words such as: First, next, then, after, last, and finally.

As students move to the upper grades and are writing essays that will be scored, they should be using transitional phrases/sequential phrases instead of transitions or sequence words. The transitional phrases students as writers use can show time of day, week, and/or year. The following is a list of strong transitional phrases that can be used for narrative, descriptive, and expository writing/essays.

In the meantime	Before we finished eating
Later that day	Later that evening
Immediately afterwards	Earlier that evening
Earlier that morning	Hours before
Moments later	Shortly afterwards
Hours later	Moments before
After we left	To begin with
Later that night	One second later

Two hours later

one year before

the next day

later that evening around 3 o'clock

soon after that

before it started raining

after the earthquake was over

soon after the sun went down

after we changed clothes

before we went swimming

after a while

after music class

moments before we left for art

from now on

at the same time

after a few days

in addition

When we finished

When we were done

After___ minutes

to put it differently (expository essay)

the next step (expository essay)

the first step (expository essay)

equally important (expository essay)

above (descriptive essay)

to the left (descriptive essay)

to the right (descriptive essay)

in the background (descriptive essay)

across the street (descriptive essay)

in a neighborhood nearby (descriptive essay)

under (descriptive essay)

Using Figurative Language

What is Figurative Language?

Figurative Language is when you describe a person or something by comparing it to something else. There are several different types of figurative language. When using figurative language in your writing, it allows the reader to see what is happening in a story or poem. Some common types of figurative language are: similes, metaphors, hyperboles, idioms, onomatopoeia, and personification. Below are some definitions and an example of these types of figurative language.

Simile

A simile uses the words "like" or "as" to compare one object or idea with another to suggest they are alike. **Example:** The man was as tall as a tree. *The man is being compared to a tree.*

Metaphor

A metaphor compares an object or idea with another *without* the words "like" or "as" and says you **are** something instead of you **are like** something. **Example:** The blanket was a cloud when I laid my face on it after an exhausting day at school. *The blanket is being compared to a cloud by saying the blanket is a cloud.*

Personification

Personification is a figure of speech in which an animal or an object is given human characteristics. **Example:** *Time flew* and before we knew it, it was time to go home.

Hyperbole

A hyperbole is an exaggeration that is so dramatic and far from the truth, that no one would believe it. **Example:** This backpack weighs a ton!

Onomatopoeia

Onomatopoeia is the use of a word to imitate or describe a sound a person, animal, or an object makes.

Example: KA-BOOM! PLOPP! BOOM!

Idiom

An idiom is an expression that has a meaning that is apart from the meaning of the actual words themselves. **Example:** It's raining cats and dogs.

Similes

As big as an elephant

As tough as leather

As busy as a bee

As proud as a peacock

As sharp as a tack

As slow as molasses

As tough as nails

As cold as ice

As black as coal

As brave as a lion

As clean as a whistle

As cute as a button

As dry as the desert

As smooth as silk

As bright as day

As bright as the sun

As sick as a dog

As quick as a cat

As snug as a bug in a rug

As easy as 1, 2, 3

As pure as snow

As white as snow

Metabphors

He has the heart of a lion

She is the sun in my sky

You are the light of my life

Her mind is a sponge

She is an early bird

The homework was a breeze

His teeth were pearly white

I am dead tired

His voice is music to my ears

Personification

The thunder clapped angrily.

The stars danced playfully in the moonlit sky.

The ray of the sun tiptoed through the meadow.

The toast jumped up out the toaster.

The fire ran wild through the forest.

The time crept up on us.

The tornado ran through the city without care.

The sun smiled down on me.

The man didn't realize that opportunity was knocking at the door.

Time flew and before the lady knew it, it was time to leave.

The sun smiled happily at us.

The bright colored car screamed for attention.

The wind howled as the hurricane hit our city.

Before he knew it, life had passed him by.

Lightning danced across the sky.

The flowers begged for water.

The camera loved the model.

The wind screamed as it raced around the building.

The wind whispered softly through the meadow.

Time does not wait for anyone.

The sun greeted us with a smile.

The moon played hide and seek with the clouds.

The snow quickly wrapped a white blanket around the city.

Hyperboles

His backpack weighs a ton.

She was so tired she could sleep for a year.

He was so hungry he could eat a horse.

His house was so cold it felt like an icebox.

The thirsty children could drink a waterfall dry.

If he asks me to dance I will die of embarrassment.

I am so busy I am doing one million things at the same time.

Her smile was a mile wide.

I have told you the same thing a million times.

I had a ton of homework.

It took two seconds to make dinner.

We waited in line for decades.

She won a ton of money.

Her truck is a million years old.

The basketball player was a thousand feet tall.

Those shoes were killing me.

The students are working their fingers to the bone.

She never stops talking.

He told the biggest tale ever.

I can smell pizza a mile away.

Her ice cream cone was a mile high.

She screamed so loud I thought my ears would explode

That was the easiest test ever!

Onomatopoeias

Buzz	Plunk
Boom	Click
Poof	Boing
Whoosh	Bong
Zoom	Flick
Squish	Bang
Splash	Clink
Crackle	Baam
Pop	Blast
Ka-boom	Pow
Plop	Hiss
Ping	

Idioms

To make ends meet: This does not literally mean forcing the ends of an object to meet. It means *to have enough money from day to day*. **Situation this idiom can be used in:** If someone is poor, they do what they have to do to be able to survive.

To get out of hand: This does not literally mean someone is holding something and it gets out of their hand. It means *for something or someone to get out of control*.
Situation this idiom can be used in: If a substitute has a classroom and all of the children started to fight.

To take someone under your wing: This does not literally mean an animal has a wing and put someone under it. *It means to be like a mentor to someone by training, helping, or looking after them.*
Situation this idiom can be used in: If a new student transfers to a school, one of the older students took the student under their wing.

To pull your weight: This does not literally mean to grab your body and pull yourself. *It means to work hard and to give equal or more help when working in or with a group of people.*
Situation this idiom can be used in: If a teacher has a group of students working on a project everyone should pull their weight.

Under the weather: Naturally we are always "under" the weather. *However, this phrase means to not feel well or to be sick.*
Situation this idiom can be used in: The teacher didn't come to school yesterday, because he was under the weather.

To throw in the towel: This doesn't mean to literally throw a towel. *It means to give up on something or someone.*
Situation this idiom can be used in: An eight year old boy tried hard to learn to ride a bike. He kept falling down so he decided to throw in the towel.

To be a piece of cake: This does not literally mean a slice of cake that you would eat. *It means something that is very easy.*
Situation this idiom can be used in: My friend said the test was hard, but I thought it was a piece of cake.

To be beat: This doesn't mean someone was hit or lost at a game or something. *It means someone who is tired and exhausted.*
Situation this idiom can be used in: I had a long day. I went to school, band practice, and played in a football game. Now I'm beat!

To bite off more than you can chew: This doesn't mean you bit off a piece of food and you could not chew it. *It means to take responsibility for more than a person can handle.*
Situation this idiom can be used in: I am really behind on my work today. I am going to ask a friend for some help. I think I bit off more than I can chew!

Instead of...

Vocabulary! Vocabulary! Vocabulary! Students should be encouraged to use vivid words and they should be provided with alternatives to overused words. List synonyms for the overused words and post lists throughout the school year. What other words can be used for large? What about hefty, humungous, colossal, or gigantic? More points are given for a misspelled word that is more sophisticated, than a safe, overused word that is spelled correctly. Teachers can have a funeral to bury those "dead" words.

Commonly overused words are listed below.

Like	Sad
Good	Walked
Smart	Laughed
Pretty	Big
Saw	Little
Funny	Said

Instead of _like_ use:	Instead of _good_ use:	Instead of _smart_ use:
love	great	witty
admire	pleasant	bright
appreciate	marvelous	quick-witted
adore	delightful	knowledgeable
idolized	amazing	intelligent
cherish	wonderful	clever
care for	splendid	ingenious
favor	superb	sharp
enjoy	grand	brainy
treasure	terrific	brilliant

Instead of _pretty_ use:	Instead of _saw_ use:	Instead of _funny_ use:
beautiful	glimpsed	farcical
lovely	noticed	jocular
glamorous	observed	amusing
attractive	sighted	humorous
elegant	spotted	witty
exquisite	stared at	comical
gorgeous	glanced at	hysterical
stunning	eyed	sidesplitting
handsome	gazed at	hilarious
striking	spied	laughable
	examined	silly
	watched	

Instead of _sad_ use:	Instead of _walked_ use:	Instead of _laughed_ use:
downcast	staggered	snickered
depressed	traveled	giggled
woeful	strutted	roared
gloomy	marched	chuckled
miserable	hiked	chortled
sorrowful	shuffled	crowed
unhappy	sauntered	guffawed
dejected	lumbered	cackled
forlorn	paraded	howled
melancholy	ample	tittered
crestfallen	strolled	hee-hawed
mournful		bellowed

Instead of _big_ use:	Instead of _little_ use:	Instead of _said_ use:
towering	teeny	called
huge	diminutive	cried
large	compact	responded
great	microscopic	demanded
gigantic	petite	asked
mammoth	wee	stated
enormous	small	shouted
tremendous	tiny	whispered
massive	minuscule	remarked
giant	miniature	questioned
colossal	slight	replied
immense		announced

Juicy Color Words

In this world we are splashed with all colors beyond our imagination. There are different shades from every color family. Juicy color words are names of *specific* colors. Good writers paint a picture in the reader's mind. One way to do that is by using specific colors to describe. Writers should be careful not to overuse these words and to make the writing sound natural. One or two of these juicy words add enough pizzazz to a writing piece.

Example: The teacher awarded the student with the best attendance a pencil.

Example (Revised sentence): The teacher awarded the student with the best attendance a shiny, **apple red** pencil.

Red	Blue	Yellow
Cherry red	powder blue	mustard yellow
Lobster red	royal blue	goldenrod
Watermelon red	navy blue	lemon yellow
Candy apple red	indigo	egg yolk yellow
Crimson red	denim blue	school bus yellow
Brick red	sapphire	fluorescent yellow
dark red	turquoise	canary
bright red		
blood red		

Green	Purple	Orange
Olive green	lavender	burnt orange
Kelly green	orchid	fluorescent orange
Pistachio green	plum	pumpkin orange
Lime green	periwinkle	marigold
Emerald green	lilac	sunset orange
Forest green	violet	apricot

Brown	Black	White
Chestnut brown	ebony	snow white
Coffee brown	jet black	alabaster white
Camel	charcoal	vanilla
Leather brown	midnight black	eggshell
Chocolate brown	pitch black	pearl
		ivory

Vivid Verbs

Blotted

       Bolted

Constructed

            Demolished

       Flattered

Groaned

              Jabbed

       Juggled

Karate chopped

         Leaped

             Manipulated

    Oozed

           Outwitted

Pasted

       Plucked

               Pounded

       Pranced

           Ransacked

Sabotaged

       Shivered

             Slithered

Splattered

        Splurged

   Squished

Strained

Awesome Adjectives

 Sight- psychedelic, textured, translucent, twisted, transparent, opaque, crystal clear, foggy, bright, cloudy, shaded, spotted, swirling, striped

 Sound- buzzing, clanking, booming, chiming, crashing, growling, howling, humming, jingling, roaring, screeching, splashing, whistling, ticking, sputtering

 Taste- buttery, cheesy, fishy, nutty, peppery, spoiled, spicy, salty, sour, stale, sugary, sweet, tart, smoky, sweet & sour, bitter, burnt

 Smell- smoky, dusty, grassy, leathery, rainy, rosy, rotten, fruity, musty, old, flowery

 Touch- brittle, furry, glassy, smooth, spongy, crusty, gooey, hairy, gritty, moist, puffy, rough, slimy, sticky

Character qualities- Educated, crafty, intelligent, foolish, irrational, trustworthy, sensible, clever, narrow-minded, honorable, idealistic, talented, wise, controversial, inspirational, absurd, superficial, humorous, dramatic, incredible, strong, vivacious, charming, elegant, deceitful, dishonorable, fascinating, horrible, clumsy, cautious, compassionate, humble

More ways to add detail

Tell more about the "who"

- What do the characters in the story look like?
- What are the characters wearing?
- How do the characters look?
- What is the character's name?
- How old is the character?
- What type of character?
    - a college student
    - a grumpy old man
    - an eight year old boy
    - a screaming baby
    - a retired teacher
    - a rich singer
    - a funny-looking fluffy dog

Tell more about the "where"

- Where is the story taking place?
    - In a barnyard
    - In the kitchen of the house
    - At an elementary school
    - At the top of an abandoned building
    - in the upstairs bedroom
    - in the forest

Tell more about the "when"

- When does the story take place?
- What was going on while the story was taking place?
    -during a forest fire
    -after an earthquake
    -before lunch
    -September 11, 2001

Add numbers

- What time?
- How much?
- What age?
- How fast?
- How many?
    -6:30a.m
    -$45.00
    -6 years old
    -80 mph
    -13 chairs

Sample School-Wide Writing Plan

August

- School-wide writing scores will be reviewed by the administrative team
- A mock writing prompt will be given within the first three weeks of the school year as a pre-test
- The administrative staff will meet to analyze the mock writing scores
- Principal will conduct classroom observations to observe daily writing instruction
- Teachers will provide writing instruction 5 days a week (P.O.W.E.R)
- Teachers will publish student work
- Students will share their writing with their peers
- Teachers develop strategies based on students final products
- Teachers will have a writing station in their classrooms
- Teachers on each grade level will have common writing time
- Teachers will create a writing portfolio for each child
- Teachers will attend a professional development workshop on the ways to implement writing and will see samples of RAFTs. (Role, Audience, Format, Topic)
- Teachers will introduce elements of a story: setting, character, resolution, & closing (by the end of the first month of school)
- Students will know how to create a/an opening/ introduction/hook

September
<ul><li>Writing coach/teacher will observe teachers during writing instruction time and provide feedback</li><li>Teachers will document weekly instructional activities</li><li>Administer weekly writing tests</li><li>School Leadership Team analyzes writing data</li><li>Teachers develop strategies based on writing scores</li><li>Students should be writing paragraphs (by the 4th week of school)</li><li>Students should be opening with strong catchy hooks (by the 5th week of school)</li><li>Students should be using proper nouns correctly in their writing (by the 6th week of school)</li><li>Students should be using quotations and dialogue correctly in their writing (by the 7th week of school)</li><li>Teachers will begin to implement the P.O.W.E.R writing routine</li></ul>

October
• Teachers will began to implement RAFT during writing instruction
• Portfolio will be checked by the administrators (every reporting period)
• Teachers will provide writing instruction 5 days a week (P.O.W.E.R)
• Teachers will publish student work
• Students will share their writing with their peers
• Students will begin to use transitional phrases in place of transition words (week 8)
• Students should be using descriptive words in their writing (week 9)
• Students should begin to use similes and metaphors in their writing (week 10)
• Students should begin to bury common words, i.e. said, went, gone, etc. (week 11)
• Students will begin to use commas w/complex sentences (week 12)

November
• Teachers will implement RAFT during writing
• Teachers will provide writing instruction 5 days a week (P.O.W.E.R)
• Teachers will publish student work
• Students will share their writing with their peers
• Students will begin to use sensory details with vivid words (week 13)
• Students will begin to use onomatopoeia in their writing

December
• Portfolio will be checked by the administrators (end of next reporting period)
• Teachers will provide writing instruction 5 days a week (P.O.W.E.R)
• Teachers will publish student work
• Students will share their writing with their peers
• Teachers will implement RAFT during writing instruction
• Students will create well developed opening statements/ paragraphs (week 14)
• Students will create well developed closing statements/ paragraphs (week 15)
• Students will use a riddle or a puzzle as a beginning sentence grabber (week 16)

January
• Teachers will provide writing instruction 5 days a week (P.O.W.E.R)
• Teachers will publish student work
• Students will share their writing with their peers
• Teachers will implement RAFT during writing instruction
• Students will be given a prompt and create a five paragraph essay within 35 minutes (week 17)
• Students will be given a prompt and create a five paragraph essay within 35 minutes (week 18)
• Students will be given a prompt and create a five paragraph essay within 35 minutes (week 19)
• Students will be given a prompt and create a five paragraph essay within 35 minutes (week 20)

February
• Teachers will provide writing instruction 5 days a week (P.O.W.E.R)
• Teachers will publish student work
• Students will share their writing with their peers
• Teachers will implement RAFT during writing instruction
• State-wide Writing Assessment (depends on the state)

March
• Portfolio will be checked by the administrators (end of report card period)
• Teachers will provide writing instruction 5 days a week (P.O.W.E.R)
• Teachers will publish student work
• Students will share their writing with their peers
• Teachers will implement RAFT during writing instruction

April
• Teachers will provide writing instruction 5 days a week (P.O.W.E.R)
• Teachers will publish student work
• Students will share their writing with their peers
• Teachers will implement RAFT during writing instruction

May
• Portfolio will be checked by the administration team (end of the school year)
• Teachers will provide writing instruction 5 days a week (P.O.W.E.R)
• Teachers will publish student work
• Students will share their writing with their peers
• Teachers will implement RAFT during writing instruction

P-Prepare Using Graphic Organizer (Monday)

O- Organize information from graphic organizer and train students using guided writing lessons (Tuesday)

W- Learning workstations (Wednesday)

E- Editing (Thursday)

R- Revise & Publish (Friday)

Sample Writing Prompts

1. Write a story about a special time or adventure you have had.

2. Imagine you woke up and you were invisible. Write a story telling about your day.

3. You walk in your school and the building is empty. The lights are off and there are no people present. Tell what you would do and tell about your day.

4. You were just told you could be anyone in the world you wanted to be. Tell who you would choose and tell about a day in your life while being this person.

5. You arrived at school and your teacher is absent. You have been told you will be the substitute teacher for the day. What did you do?

6. You are walking home late at night and decided to take a short cut through a cemetery. Describe your experience.

7. Pretend you are a snowflake during a blizzard. For that day you get to go where snowflakes go. Think about what you would do during your day as a snowflake. Now write a story about your adventures as a snowflake in a snowstorm.

8. You are home alone babysitting your baby sister. You hear a knock at the door and you go to answer it. You don't see

anyone so you step outside into the yard to look around. All of a sudden you hear the doors shut and lock and your baby sister is in the house alone. Tell what you will do.

9. Your classroom's pet rabbit got loose inside your school. Tell about what happened.

10. Everyone in your family goes on vacation every year. This year everyone traveled to Paris, France. You fell asleep on the plane during the flight. When you wake up, all of your family members have already gotten off the plane in Paris. You get off and can't find anyone of your family members inside the airport. The cell phones do not work in Paris and you have no way of getting in contact with anyone. What did you do? Tell about your vacation in Paris.

11. Imagine you just found a pair of magic shoes. With these shoes you can go anywhere you choose. Write a story about your adventure.

12. You are in Florida swimming in the ocean. All of a sudden you see a shark swimming closer and closer to you. Tell how you feel and what you decided to do.

13. You called the radio station and won a contest. You win an all expense paid trip to spend a day with your favorite celebrity! What celebrity did you choose, what did you all do, and where did you go? Write a story describing your experience.

14. You are in charge of planning a field trip for your class. Where would you go, why, and what would you do?

Sample Essays

(Student A)

Have you ever been to the Mid-south Fair? Well I have!! When I first got there I was amazed!!!

When I first got there I rode rides, I rode the Roller coaster first. As I got on I looked down and fainted. I didn't even know where my parents were. So the ride was moving and we didn't know when it was going to drop. So I closed my eyes. I knew the hill was coming. As we went down my stomach felt weaker and weaker. We were going really fast as I shouted "Momma!" I threw up on the people next to me. They screamed, "Yuck!!" as the ride ended.

I was trudging as I was walking. We rode the bumper cars. As I got on people were staring at me because I looked nasty. When we started I got bumped in the back of the bumper car! I screamed, "Dog!", but that was a part of the bumper cars. So I was looking for the one that bumped me and someone else bumped me! I said, "Forget this!" When that happened I bumped someone with a blue black shiny car. After I hit it...it wasn't shiny anymore. Five minutes later, it was the end of the bumper cars.

About an hour later my stomach started to growl. So I told my mom. We went to the area where food was. I got a hot chicken on a stick and a funnel cake with a lot of powder on it. As we sat down on the blackberry beautiful table, the funnel cake was as sweet as a bag of sugar!! The funnel cake was crispy as toast!!

An hour later, I played games. First I played basketball. As I realized the ball wasn't a girls' ball so I thought, "It doesn't matter." As I got the ball she told me to step up on this yellow banana colored line.

So I said, "I'm fine." She responded, "Are you sure?" I replied, "Yes." As I shot I made it as everybody was shocked!! So I decided I should get in the dunk tank. As my sister through the ball I knew she was going to hit the target. Then I dropped in the cold blue water and it was cold as snow. After that I said, "I'm not getting in anymore!!"

Before we left I met a friend. They were nice, as I told them my name. They replied with their names. I said, "Well, nice to meet you." I asked them would they like to visit. They said, "Sometime this year."

I felt sad as I left the Mid- South Fair. I begged my parents could I stay and they said, "No!!" I didn't want to talk back so I just said, "Yes Maam."

Buzz! Buzz! My alarm went off as I woke up and slipped out of bed. My mom told me we were going to the fair today at two o'clock p.m.

When we first got there I rushed to the scary, metal roller coaster. When I was on the ride my stomach had butterflies in it and everybody had held on to the bars stronger than Mr. T picking up weights. After that ride I ran to the Ferris wheel and got in line. As I got on I was calm as a dove flying. We went up, down, up, and down.

After the rides I took a break and ate a good, creamy, funnel cake. The people around me stared as I ate the delicious funnel cake. Five minutes later, I got thirsty and hot so I bought a strawberry slushy so I could eat and drink at the same time. When the slushy went to my stomach I felt good and unstressed.

A half hour later, I went to play some mini-games like basketball. I walked to the booth and played. I was like Michael Jordan in the booth. Everybody was jealous. The next mini-game I played was dunk tank. The person in the dunk tank said, "You can't hit me, you're too weak." I got angry and threw it with all of my might. "Splash", he hits the water. He came out soaking wet. I hollered, "Who's weak now?" Everybody clapped as I left the area.

After thirty minutes I saw my friend and principal, Mr. Jones. We stopped and socialized with her. I told her that she was a good socialize. My mom, my little sister, Mr. Jones, and I after about fifteen minutes of walking met up with Mrs. Boyd, my fifth grade teacher. She looked energized and hyper. She told me that she was drinking too much soda. I said, "That's why you're hyper!" "Yes!" she screamed. She left and went to the rides and I left towards the exit gate.

As I left, I cried hard and screamed, "I don't want to go home!" I started to cool down as I got home at night. "Wow!' I said, "Look at the stars upon the night sky." As I looked up, I felt sleepy and I was. "ZZZZZZZZZ", as I slept.

"Wow!" my brother shouted "Yippee," I said as we ran to the roller coaster. But just so you will know we go every single year on Mondays.

When I first got there, I rode on rides. The first ride I got on was the Super Man. When it started it was so scary. So, when I got off I went to the Batman. It was so fun!

After that we went to the food counter. When we got to the food counter I still felt dizzy. I ate turkey legs and funnel cakes. It tasted so good. I just wanted to fall out it was so good!

An hour later we played games. My big brother asked, "Can we go to the basketball games?" Then my mom said, "Yes." So next we went and played on the orange and blue basketball goal. At last we went to the dunk tank. When the other kids dunked I got soaked with icy cold water.

Before we left we met up with my best friends Calvin and Miyah. They asked, "Are you here by yourself?" I replied, "No." "Oh, okay let's go ride the ring of fire", they said. It was fun but scary at the same time.

But when it was time to go I didn't want to go. So then I got mad! And as we walked out I got as quiet as a mouse. But we are going to go back next year. And that was an awesome day.

Have you ever been to the Mid-South Fair? Well I have. I went with my family last Friday. We go every year so why not go this year?

When we first got there my family and I decided to ride the rides first. We strolled our way to the Ultimate Roller Coaster, Coaster X. As Coaster X went up the steep hill to the glimmering night sky, everyone on the roller coaster screamed, "Aaaa Ahhh!" The coaster rushed down, upside down, around, and around. Soon I got off the roller coaster feeling cozy. Two seconds later, I threw up on everybody and hustled to the bumper cars. Finally I was next in line. I got in a green, yellow, and red bumper car. Then this old man came up and hit me in the back bumper. "Old man you wanna play?" I scoldingly asked him.

After that, I got off the bumper cars and rushed toward the food stands. As I walked down the street I smelled all the different fragrances, they smelled so delicious. That made me hungry. I ran towards the juicy, yellow, steamy corn on the cob. Immediately, I saw my cousin Brandon. I shouted, "Brandon, come eat some corn with me!" He replied with a scream, "No, you are lame!" I scolded, "You're a big meanie!" After that, I was still hungry so I ate a corn dog and it was delicious.

An hour later, we were walking and I felt the need to play some games. So I played catch the Ducky. I had the fishing rod in my hands. I brought it back over my shoulders and threw the fishing rod in my hands. I brought it back over my shoulders and threw it into a pond. Quack, quack I had caught the ducky. For my prize I picked up a white tiger. I went on to the next game. "Who wants to play basketball?" the clerk asked. I replied, "Me!" I missed every shot.

Before we left, I met a new friend. His name is Doofenmirtz Evil. We walked on then I saw my friend Edwardsan. My friends, my family, and I left the fair. We had the greatest time ever. Will you go next time?

Did you know that the Mid-South Fair has been in Memphis since the mid 1850's? Well, September 2008 I attended.

When I first got there, I bumbled over to rides. The first ride I got on was the Yo-yo. When the ride started so did my stomach. I got very nervous. Finally, the ride stopped. Next, I rushed over to the water slide, so I could get there first. While I was on the ride I got soak and wet, but I had fun.

After that, I went to the food court down the street. They had funnel cakes, corn dogs, hot dogs, and popcorn. The first thing I ate was a hot dog. Immediately, I went to the funnel cake stand. They had all kinds like lemon powder, strawberry powder, orange powder, and my personal favorite sugar powder.

A few minutes later, I went to play games. I walked over to the strength contest. I was one more notch away from being the strongest, but won second place. Next, I went to the museum they had way in the back. I bought a new glow in the dark bracelet.

Before I left, I met my friends. First, I saw Kristina and we talked for a while. Next, I saw Johona and we talked even longer. Finally, I saw Erica and we talked even longer than before.

I was sad that I had to leave. I wonder if I will see more of my friends next year.

Sample Mini-Lessons

Mini-lessons should be short, focused, and modeled by the teacher. Mini-lessons should be taught 2-3 times a week.

Focus: Effective openings
Teacher can read various books to students and have students to listen for different types of beginnings/openings. Teacher and students can identify these and list them on the board. The students can identify what type of hook is used.

Focus: Effective endings
Teacher can read various books to students and have students to listen for different types of endings. Teacher and students can identify these and list them on the board. The students can identify what type of ending is used.

Focus: Figurative language
Teacher can read various books to students and have students to listen for different types of figurative language. Teacher and students can identify these and list them on the board. They can also write them on sentence strips and post them on the board. After that, the teacher can guide students in sorting them by the type of figurative language it is.

Focus: Main Idea
Teacher can have several topic sentences/main ideas written on sentence strips. The teacher will have several sentences displayed that relate to one of the topic sentences. The teacher reads all the sentences with the students and they discuss what they have in common. Students will decide which supporting details go with the correct topic sentence/main idea.

Focus: Supporting details
Teacher can have several sentences that are supporting details for a particular topic written on sentence strips. The teacher will have several topic sentences displayed that relate to various sentences. The teacher reads all the supporting details along with the students and they discuss what the sentences have in common. Students will decide which topic sentence goes with the correct supporting details.

Focus: Varied descriptive words
The teacher will have a sample essay displayed that uses too many "tired" overused words. The students along with the teacher will replace those words with varied descriptive words.

Focus: Well thought out openings
Teacher will give students a prompt. The teacher will remind the students of having a well thought out opening. The teacher will guide students on focusing on identifying who, did what, when, where, and why for the prompt. After this, students will use this information to create an opening that includes a hook.

Sample "scripted" writing lesson

Here I have provided a detailed "scripted" lesson sample. I only showed how you will scaffold a lesson with the introduction. This shows what the teacher and students may say during a writing lesson. The prompt and situation is provided.

Prompt: Imagine you had the best birthday ever. Tell about your day.

Directions: Think about where you went, who was there, what you did, and when you went. Tell about how your day went.

Teacher: So now that you know what your prompt is, what is the first thing you should do.

Various Students' responses

Teacher: Ok. Everyone gave great responses. The first thing you should do is brainstorm. So let's think about the prompt. Can you all think of a time you had the best birthday party?

Students respond

Teacher: Great! Let's write about the time you went to Disney World for your birthday. What are some of the things you do and see when you go to Disney World? Even if you never have been to Disney World before, you can still think of some things you do if you go there.

Student A: You ride rides.

Student B: You see Disney characters.

Student C: Buy souvenirs

Student D: Eat

Student E: Go to concerts

Student F: You play games.

Teacher: All of those answers are awesome, but when we are writing a story, you need to narrow it down and choose only three events you are going to discuss when brainstorming. Let's choose riding rides, eating food, and seeing your favorite Disney Characters. Now that we have brainstormed and we have our three events, we need to give your readers more details. What ride did you ride? Did you ride a roller coaster, bumper cars, water logs, or the ferris wheel?

Student: A roller coaster

Teacher: Let's talk about when you rode the roller coaster. Now let's write that down on our planning guide or graphic organizer.

Teacher: Now let's pick one food item that you want to talk about eating?

Student A: Corn dog

Student B: popcorn

Student C: candy apples

Student D: pizza

Student E: hot wings

Student F: funnel cake

Teacher: Great! Now let's write funnel cake down. What Disney

Character do you want to tell your audience more about? Think about your favorite Disney Character.

Student A: "Winnie the Pooh!"

Student B: "Goofy!"

Student C: "Donald Duck!"

Student D: "Mickey Mouse!"

Teacher: You are on the right track! Since we are only focusing on one Disney Character, let's write about Mickey Mouse.

Teacher: Now children, we now have our three events we will write about. We are going to write about riding a roller coaster, eating funnel cake, and seeing Mickey Mouse. Each one of the events will represent a paragraph in our essay. Let's continue to brainstorm and think about our introductory statements. First we will decide who will be in the story, when it will take or took place, where it is going to or where it took place, and why. All of these questions should be answered in our introduction which is our first paragraph. Let's think about that.

Teacher: *Who* is going to be in your story?

Student: My mom, my dad, my sister & brother, and me.

Teacher: Ok. *Where* did the story take place? Now we already know at Disney World for our "where", but we can be even more specific. Where is Disney World?

Student: In Orlando, Florida.

Teacher: Exactly! *When* can we say the story take place?

Student A: Last summer

Student B: June 21, 2011

Student C: During our family reunion.

Student D: Three years ago

Student E: When I was eight years old.

Teacher: Those are great answers! There are so many ways to describe when a story is taking place.

Teacher: *Why* did you go to Disney World?

Student: To celebrate my birthday.

Teacher: Don't forget, we don't want to start our story with "Once upon a time". That is boring and it is expected of young writers. We want to spice our writing up with the unexpected and hold the reader's attention. So we are going to do this by starting with a hook. Who can give me some hooks I can use?

Student A: We can start with a question.

Student B: We can start with dialogue.

Student C: I can start with suspense.

Student D: An extraordinary fact.

Student E: I looked at my list of hooks you gave us and chose, "Was it something I ate, something I drank, a wish upon a star?"

Teacher: You all are really thinking today! Let's use the suspense hook this time. This will grab our reader's attention and get them sitting on the edge of their seats to see what is going to happen! Can anyone think of a statement we can use for suspense?

Students respond (teacher will assist in prompting and probing the students to get them to think critically and creatively of a statement of suspense.)

Teacher: So let's write that statement on the board. "My eyes grew bigger and bigger as the ride climbed higher and higher to the top."

Teacher: Does anyone see one of those "tired", "dead", and "overused" words?

Student: Yes! Bigger!

Teacher: What word can I replace bigger with?

Student: Tremendous

Student: Enormous

Student: Gigantic

Teacher: Ok. Those are some great responses. Let's replace bigger with more enormous.

Teac her: Who can help me come up with the next part? It sounds like the narrator is going up a roller coaster. What can happen next? Can someone help me with the next sentence?

Student A: You can throw up.

Student B: You can get scared.

Student C: The cart came loose, opened, and someone fell out.

Teacher: I like that! Let's choose only one of those, make it sound interesting, and make sure we are giving details with clear descriptions. We want our reader to be able to paint a picture in their minds as they are reading our stories. Keep in mind when you add more details, you want to use the five main questions in mind. *What were you doing, what were the people around you doing, what were you thinking, what were you feeling, and describe the setting.* If you answer these questions, they will guide your writing from one sentence to another. Don't forget to let the reader know how things smell, what things sound like, how it looks, and how it feels. So watch me and listen as I spice those statements up.

Teacher: *"My eyes grew more and more enormous as the ride climbed higher and higher to the top."*

All of a sudden, I heard a loud rattle coming from the cart I was riding in. "Cling!", "Cling!", swung the latch to the cart. My heart rapidly pounded like thunder. I glanced down to see the people trotting around anxiously. They appeared to be tiny ants from my view above. "Oh no!" I shouted. "What's wrong?" asked the man in the cart with me. "Our cart came unlatched!" I replied. He quickly reached over and locked it as I sighed heavily with relief. Last summer my family and I traveled to Disney World in Orlando, Florida. It was my mom, my dad, my brother, and me. They surprised me for my 8th birthday! Let me tell you all about my adventure!

Teacher: Students notice we didn't use said. Why didn't we use said?

Students: Said is dead!

Student A: Said is dead and it isn't interesting. It is expected of students to use the word said.

Teacher: Great job! Notice we used a hook, figurative language, dialogue, and set the scene for our reader. We grabbed their attention by getting them hooked to what our story was about. We included who, did what, when, where, and why. Now I am going to let you finish the rest of the story on your own and I will come around and give you feedback. Don't forget to use transitional phrases to show you are moving from one event to the next. Let's get started!

Sample Graphic Organizers

PLAN! PLAN! PLAN! All good writers plan, brainstorm, and jot down their ideas before they start to write. Below are examples of graphic organizers that can be used to plan.

- Introductory statement
- Use a hook
- Use figurative language
- Use dialogue
- State the main events (3)

TP, 1st event, supporting details using figurative language, dialogue, & the 5 w's.	TP, 2nd event, supporting details using figurative language, dialogue, & the 5 w's.	TP, 3rd event, supporting details using figurative language, dialogue, & the 5 w's.

- Closing paragraph beginning with a transitional phrase
- Wrap up the story and don't use: THE END, THIS IS THE END OF MY STORY, I WENT HOME, I WENT TO SLEEP, or I WENT TO BED
- End with a feeling telling how you felt about the entire story.

TP= transitional phrase

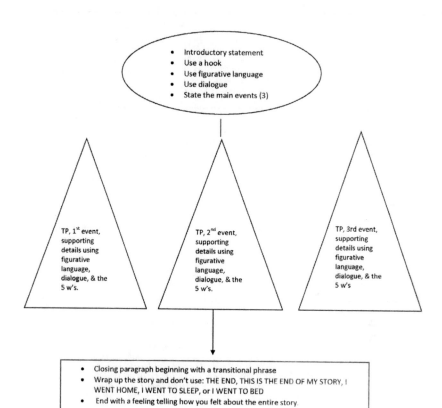

- Introductory statement
- Use a hook
- Use figurative language
- Use dialogue
- State the main events (3)

TP, 1st event, supporting details using figurative language, dialogue, & the 5 w's.

TP, 2nd event, supporting details using figurative language, dialogue, & the 5 w's.

TP, 3rd event, supporting details using figurative language, dialogue, & the 5 w's

- Closing paragraph beginning with a transitional phrase
- Wrap up the story and don't use: THE END, THIS IS THE END OF MY STORY, I WENT HOME, I WENT TO SLEEP, or I WENT TO BED
- End with a feeling telling how you felt about the entire story.

Essay Rough Draft

Essay Rough Draft

Essay Rough Draft

Essay Rough Draft

Essay Rough Draft

Essay Rough Draft

Essay Rough Draft

Essay Rough Draft

Essay Rough Draft

Essay Rough Draft

CPSIA information can be obtained at www.ICGtesting.com
Printed in the USA
LVOW110541090512

280906LV00004B/61/P